Strong Women

Congresswoman Carolyn B. Maloney

Illustrations by Emily Cicora

DI ANGELO PUBLICATIONS
A Modernized Publishing Firm

One evening I took a stroll through Central Park, and suddenly a thought crossed my mind that just couldn't be.

I noticed that of the abundance of statues in the city, important women were often left out, though they trailblazed paths for you and me.

Sometimes forgotten in history books and museum displays we have today, their stories must be told—these ladies truly paved the way.

So I sat on a park bench and began to jot down some more women who were influential.

I wanted to make sure that girls today know they can reach their full potential.

OLGA MÉNDEZ

In 1972, Olga Méndez was a groundbreaking politician.

She was the first Puerto Rican woman to hold a New York Senate position.

Born to an educated family where hard work was nothing new,

She brought her skills to the United States, home of the red, white and blue.

Olga wanted what was best for this nation and served on many important boards,

Laying a strong foundation for other women to work towards.

She worked to bring together different sides and points of view,

Proving that collaboration created things beautiful and new.

SALLY RIDE

Sally Ride took a flight to the moon in 1983.

She made history as the first American woman in space when many people thought it couldn't be.

She was as smart as she was brave and the only woman on her team,

Living proof that women are equal and can fulfill their biggest dream!

She was a scientist and a professor, teaching physics at university,

Further demonstrating her great capability.

She worked on a robotic arm for the STS-7 space mission,

Releasing satellites into space, she was quite the skilled technician.

Don't let anyone tell you that you can't go to outer space.

Sally proved it could be done with dignity, intelligence, and grace.

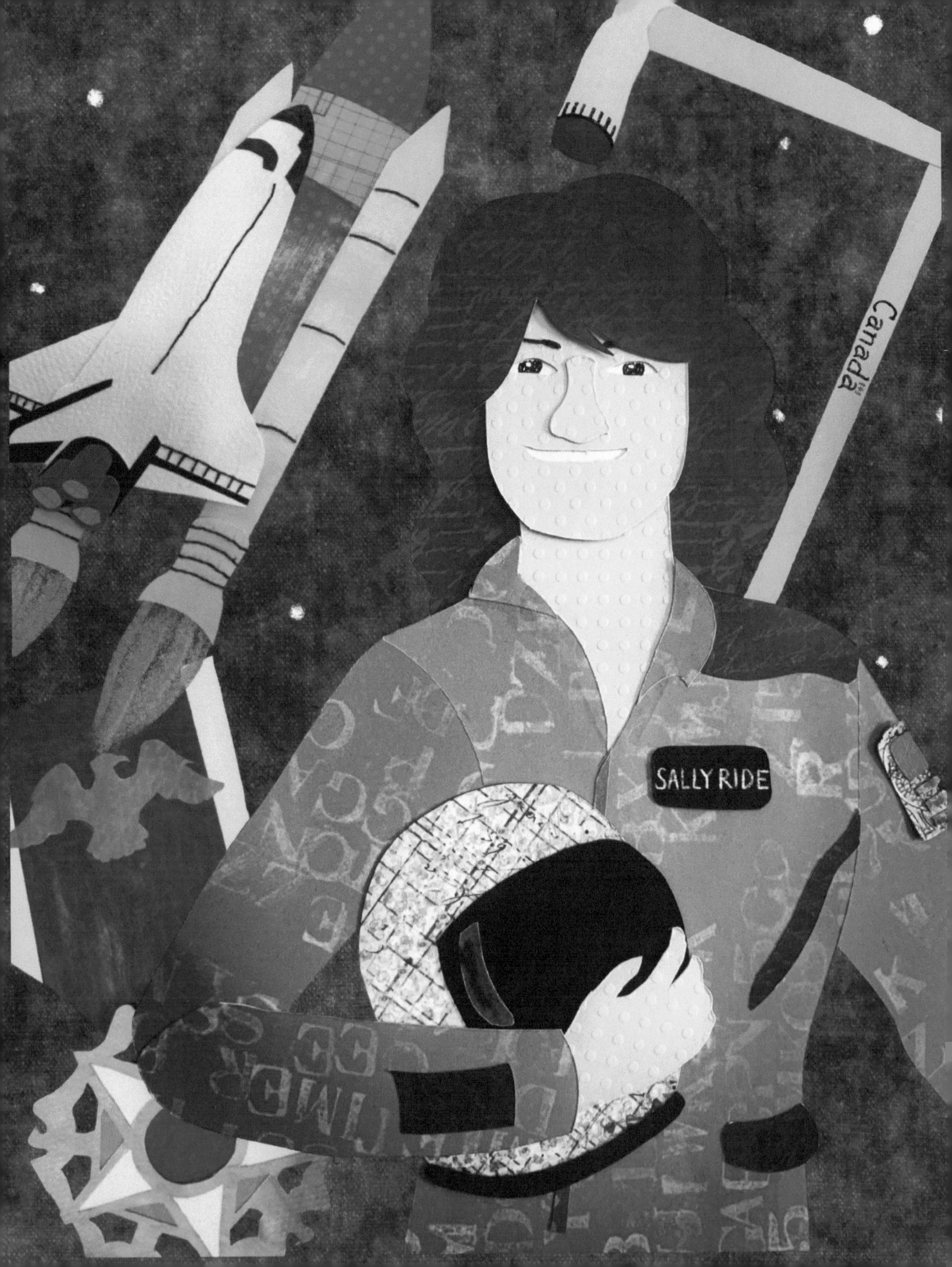

Canada
SALLY RIDE

NANCY WARD

Nanyehi in Cherokee means "One Who Goes About".

Known to Americans as Nancy Ward, a Beloved Woman of the Cherokee tribe she was, without a doubt.

Beloved Woman means she was important and held great responsibilities in her tribe.

She believed in the tribes keeping hold of their land fighting with a passion no one could describe.

Immigrants from Europe and Native Americans fought each other and invaded,

But Ward believed in peace for all, an idea for which she advocated.

She also introduced the Cherokee to the dairy farming ways.

Nancy truly helped everyone, proving kindness and hard work pays.

ELIZABETH CADY STANTON

Born in 1815, Elizabeth Cady Stanton always loved to learn.

She went to school with many boys when education for girls wasn't much of a concern.

Her father was a lawyer, judge, and Congressman so she learned all about unequal laws,

Stanton devoted her life to women and formed organizations that also supported her gender's voting cause.

She was the first woman to ever run for Congress, doing so proved that she was truly dauntless.

A prized author of her time, she encouraged other women not to fall in line.

Because her strong ideas and opinions were so evident,

She became the National Woman Suffragette Association president.

Her best friend, Susan B. Anthony, also fought for women's rights.

The path these best friends created eventually took to new and amazing heights.

JOINT RESOLU
Proposing an amendment to the Constitution extending
to women.
"The right of citizens of the United States to vote shall not be denied or abridged by the United States or by any State on account of sex.
VOTES
FOR
MEI
MR. PRESIDEN
HOW LONG
MUST
WOMEN WAIT
FOR LIBERTY

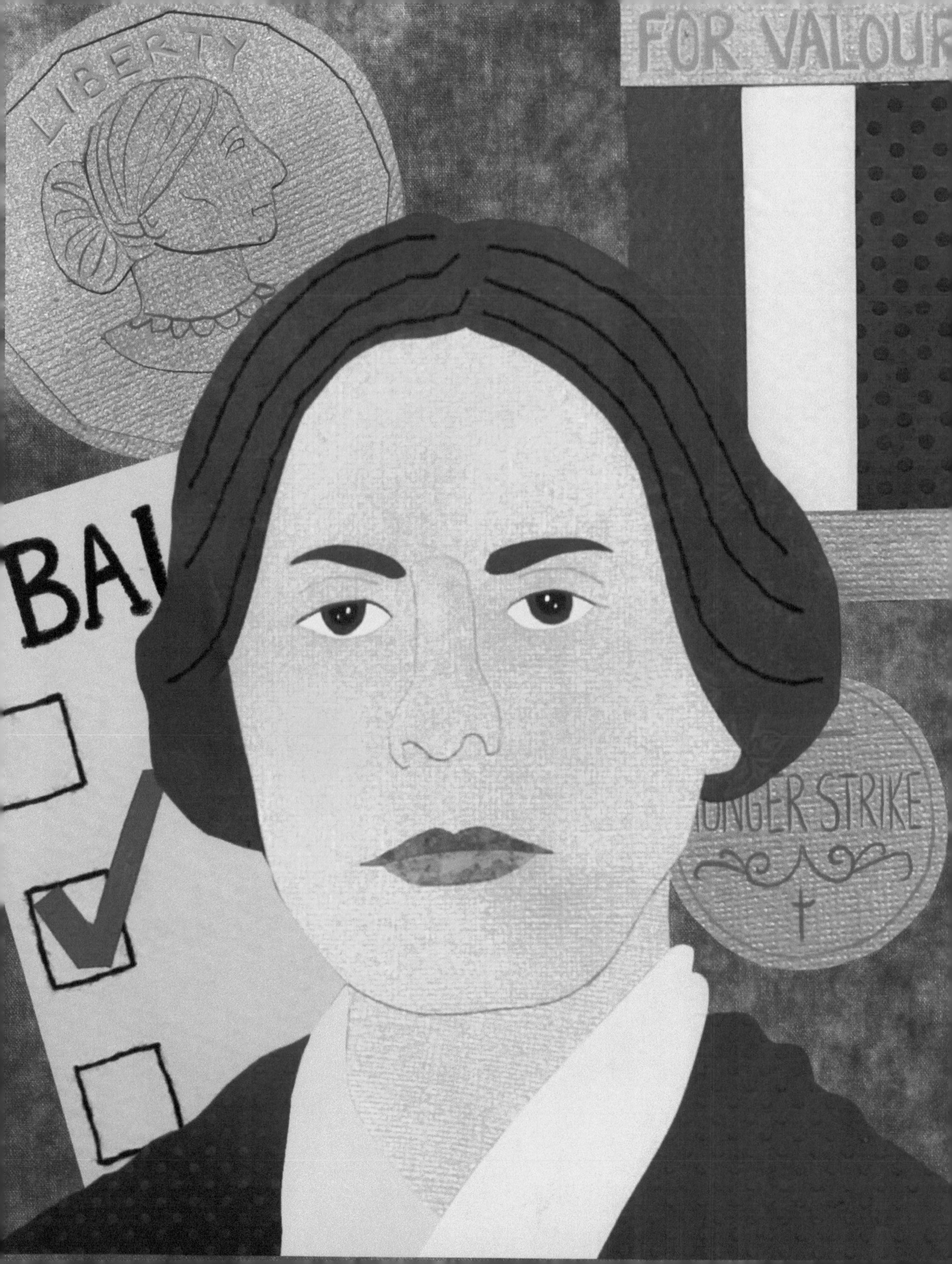
LIBERTY
FOR VALOUR
BAL
UNGER STRIKE

SUSAN B. ANTHONY

Susan B. Anthony was an influential person who helped mold female rights.

She devoted her life to help other women and put up many fights.

She wanted ladies to be equal to men in elections and the workplace.

She spent many years working on this no matter the obstacles she had to face.

Susan, along with Elizabeth Cady Stanton, founded the National Woman Suffrage Association in 1869.

It is through this organization that women's rights began to shine.

In 1872 Susan illegally cast her ballot in an election.

She was fined $100 for voting and faced many years of rejection.

Long after Anthony's death, she finally won her fight.

In 1920 an amendment was added to the constitution, making women's voting a right.

ALICE COACHMAN

Alice Coachman dreamed of being an athlete,

Long before she ever had shoes on her feet.

She ran barefoot on dirt roads outside,

So she could prove to the world she could compete with pride.

Coachman never let race or gender force her to slow down,

She practiced and trained until the Olympics came around.

She worked her hardest and competed in London in 1948,

Being the first female African American to win a gold medal was her ultimate fate.

High jump was the event that she won to get the gold,

Teaching people everywhere to not hold back and to be bold.

Coachman gave back to all the people in financial need,

She created a track and field foundation to help other young girls succeed.

NATIONAL WOMEN'S HALL OF FAME

#METOO

"THERE ARE SOME PEOPLE WHO STILL FEEL THREATENED BY STRONG WOMEN. THAT'S THEIR PROBLEM. IT'S NOT MINE.

GLORIA ALLRED

Strong, brave and smart is all part of Gloria Allred's art.

She's not average nor mediocre, and always has "the woman" at heart.

Gloria is an attorney and never hides behind a shield.

She's a fierce, fighting woman, deserving praise within her field.

In the courtroom, she argues cases for women, even when it's extremely intense.

Without her help, many women would not have any form of defense.

An activist since the 1970s, often on controversial ground,

If girls today stand up like Gloria, more strong women will abound.

SYBIL LUDINGTON

During the American Revolutionary War at the age of just 16,

Sybil Ludington took her horse, Star, on a daring night ride, careful to not be seen.

She rode fast into the dark to warn the militia of a coming British attack,

Knowing that once she took off into the night, there was no turning back.

She shouted, "The British are burning Danbury!" to help the soldiers out,

A warning that saved them, without a doubt!

She rode much further than Paul Revere on his famous ride,

She made her journey over twice as far, making sure the militia could abide.

Never receiving credit for her ride for over one hundred years,

We all respect her now for her bravery and ability to confront fears.

WALKER
THEATRE
MADAM CJ WALKER, MFG CO
MADAM C.J. WALKER'S
WONDERFUL HAIR GROWER
MADE BY
THE MADAM C J WALKER
MANUFACTURING Cº
PRICE 50 CENTS

MADAM C.J. WALKER

Madam C.J. Walker was a self-made millionaire.

Her parents died when she was a child, leaving her an orphan without care.

She was the first child in her family born free of slavery.

However, life was not easy, she had to rely on strength and bravery.

As she grew up, an awful disease caused her to lose her hair.

But she turned this into an opportunity that she would gladly share.

After researching, she made a product that cured her disease and kept her hair healthy.

Her business took off! She made more and more, and became incredibly wealthy!

The small business started out door to door before it swept the entire nation.

A woman of perseverance and determination, she is worthy of celebration. Madam C.J. Walker also helped build dreams and aspirations.

She created many jobs and opportunities, and gave scholarships and donations.

Without her work we might not have the hair care industry we have today.

Madam C.J. Walker created a legacy that's here to stay.

GABRIELLE "GABBY" GIFFORDS

Gabby studied hard in college after her admission.

She was born and raised in Arizona, and went on to be a politician.

One day while giving a special speech,

Giffords was shot by a man with a gun, and she was just within his reach!

Nineteen people were hit by bullets and six did not survive.

Giffords was rescued by her intern, who performed first aid to help keep her alive.

She had to learn how to walk, talk, read and write all over again.

Her strength and perseverance did not let the gunman win.

Giffords became an advocate for the anti gun-violence cause.

She started a foundation that's pro gun-control laws.

While still recovering, she watched her husband in the final flight of the Space Shuttle Endeavour.

Giffords' strength, activism, and amazing comeback will remain with America forever.

STRONG WOMEN GET THINGS DONE

USS GABRIELLE GIFFORDS

HENRIETTA LACKS

A hero to many, Henrietta Lacks was born in Virginia in 1920.

She discovered a strange bump inside her body and suddenly became very tired and sickly.

The doctors at Johns Hopkins Hospital worked very hard to try and heal her quickly.

Unfortunately, through many trials, the doctors couldn't find a cure.

Cancer took over her body, and it was too much for her to endure.

Yet through her diagnosis, scientists discovered that she had immortalized cells.

These cells are magnificently special for science, and her legacy still prevails.

Her body, her illness, and her death helped science to move along.

The HeLa cells, named after her, are still working and going strong.

VALERIE PLAME

Valerie Plame is a former officer of the CIA.

That means her job was to get information that helps the country in a very secret way.

Her missions included stopping people from building nuclear bombs.

Her work was very important, she didn't have any qualms.

She worked for the CIA for many years until 2003.

That's when someone revealed who she was and ruined her secret identity.

Because a person did this to her, it put her and her family in danger.

It is unfortunate that someone blew her cover out of their own anger.

It jeopardized every person who worked on her top-secret missions.

Revealing who she was put many people in life-threatening positions.

She is now an author of a memoir, spy novels, and a busy mom and wife,

But because her job as a spy was revealed, she had to start a whole new life.

There are many more brave women who work under cover like Valerie Plame,

But because of their top-secret security, we will never know their name.

SOJOURNER
TRUTH

SUSAN B.
ANTHONY

ELIZABETH CADY
STANTON

WOMEN'S RIGHTS PIONEERS

As the sun went down in the park and the city lights began to glimmer,

I tucked my notebook away and began on a path to a statue that does shimmer.

These three women are the first in the park that aren't from a fairy tale,

Proving that girls anywhere can achieve their dreams without fail.

Thanks to these pioneers, the power of women is no longer understated.

It made me think of how in the future, more women will be celebrated.

IMAGINE BOOKS

Di Angelo Publications
Creative Headquarters
4265 San Felipe #1100
Houston, Texas, 77027
Ph: (713) 960-6636

Di Angelo Distributions
Distribution Warehouse
250 Main Ave N
Twin Falls, ID 83301
Ph: (208) 969-9814

www.diangelopublications.com

Library of Congress cataloging-in-publications data
Strong Women. Downloadable via Kindle, iBooks and NOOK.

Library of Congress Registration

Hardback

ISBN: 978-1-942549-88-8

Cover Design: Savina Deianova
Words: Lindsay Ray Wright
Line Editing: Ashley Crantas
Developmental Editing: Elizabeth Geeslin Zinn
Proofing: Stephanie Yoxen
Illustrations: Emily Cicora
Interior Layout: Kim James

For educational, business and bulk orders, contact sales@diangelopublications.com.
Di Angelo Publications' authors are available for speaking engagements, seminars, and private bookings.
For information please contact info@diangelopublications.com.

1. Juvenile Nonfiction --- Biography & Autobiography --- Women
2. Juvenile Nonfiction --- History --- United States
3. History --- Women
4. History --- United States --- General
United States of America with int. Distribution.

CPSIA information can be obtained
at www.ICGtesting.com
Printed in the USA
LVHW070242070821
694728LV00003B/27